Cambridge English Readers

Starter Level

Series editor: Philip Prowse

A Death in Oxford

Richard MacAndrew

D1113569

CAMBRIDGE
UNIVERSITY PRESS

CAMBRIDGE UNIVERSITY PRESS
Cambridge, New York, Melbourne, Madrid, Cape Town, Singapore, São Paulo

Cambridge University Press
The Edinburgh Building, Cambridge CB2 8RU, UK

www.cambridge.org
Information on this title: www.cambridge.org/9780521704649

First published 2007

Richard MacAndrew has asserted his right to be identified as the Author of the Work in
accordance with the Copyright, Design and Patents Act 1988.

Printed in India by Thomson Press (India) Limited

Illustrations by Paul Dickinson

A catalogue record of this book is available from the British Library.

ISBN 978-0-521-70464-9 paperback
ISBN 978-0-521-70465-6 paperback plus audio CD pack

Contents

People in the story

Frank Williams
a police inspector

Kate Miller
a police sergeant

Jenkins
a police scientist

Janet Leighton
a doctor

Barbara Collins
a doctor at Janet
Leighton's clinic

Elizabeth Morgan
Janet Leighton's
lawyer

Simon Leighton
Janet Leighton's
husband

Chris Leighton
Janet Leighton's son

Places in the story

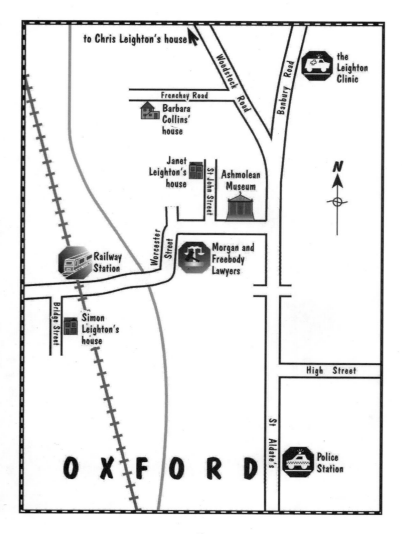

Chapter 1   *Friday 26 July: 6.30 am*

It's six thirty in the morning. Inspector Frank Williams of the Oxford police is in bed. He hears his phone and answers it.

'Williams,' he says.

'It's Kate Miller, Inspector. I'm at 17B St John Street, the house of a Dr Janet Leighton. She's dead.'

'I'm coming,' says Williams. 'Give me fifteen minutes.'

At six forty-five Williams walks into the front room of

a tall house on St John Street. He stops. There are books and papers everywhere, and a body next to the coffee table.

Sergeant Kate Miller is by the window. She's waiting for him. There's a police scientist in the room too.

'What's all this?' asks Williams.

'Someone wanting money or things to sell, I think,' says Miller. 'This is Dr Leighton's computer table – but there's no computer. And there's her bag.'

Williams looks down at the body. It's the body of a fifty-year-old woman: dark trousers and a white shirt, with a lot of red.

Miller speaks again: 'And there's this.' In her hand is a bag, and in the bag is a knife.

'Ah,' says Williams. He looks slowly at the room again. He looks at the Chinese dog. He turns it over.

'What do you think, Sergeant?' he asks.

'Someone gets into the house to take things,' she says. 'Dr Leighton tries to stop them, but maybe there's a knife on the table and …' She stops speaking.

Williams says nothing for a minute. He looks at the Chinese dog again.

'I don't know,' says Williams.

He turns to the police scientist. 'Jenkins,' he says, 'can I have a photograph of this dog?'

'OK, Inspector,' says the scientist.

Williams looks at the book on the coffee table.

'*Our Beautiful World.*' He reads the name of the book. 'Photographs from all over the world.'

There's a receipt by the book. He looks at that.

'It's a new book, too,' he says.

Next, Williams looks at the papers on the computer table. One is a letter. He reads it.

'Interesting,' he says. 'It's about Dr Leighton's will, from her lawyer. I want to know about her will. Now she's dead, who gets her money? A husband? Children?'

Miller comes over and reads the letter.

'The lawyer's name is Elizabeth Morgan, of Morgan and Freebody Lawyers,' she says. 'We can talk to her this morning.'

'Yes,' says Williams, 'but first I want to see a Dr Barbara Collins.' Miller looks at Williams, but he turns to the scientist. 'Jenkins, can you come and see me this afternoon?'

'OK, Inspector,' says the scientist.

'You can tell me all about this room then,' says Williams. 'And about the knife.'

Williams turns to Miller: 'OK, Sergeant, we can go.'

'Who's Dr Barbara Collins?' asks Miller. Williams and Miller are in Williams' car. They're driving up the Woodstock Road. It's a beautiful Oxford street with trees and houses to the left and the right.

'You're new in Oxford, I know,' says Williams. 'But don't you read the *Oxford Post*?'

'I don't have time,' answers Miller.

Williams turns left into Frenchay Road and stops in front of a big house.

He looks at Miller and smiles.

'Well, a lot of people in Oxford know Dr Collins ... and Dr Leighton.'

Chapter 2   *Thursday 25 July: 9.30 am*

Barbara Collins' story

'What's this?' asks Barbara Collins angrily. She's a tall woman with long dark hair. There's a paper in her hand. It's the *Oxford Post*. She reads from it.

Journalist Darren Atkinson speaks to Dr Janet Leighton, of the Leighton Clinic on Banbury Road.

'The clinic is having a bad time, but we're not closing,' says Dr Leighton. 'Clinics are expensive and we always need money. This year we're asking some of our doctors to leave.'

One of these doctors is Dr Barbara Collins. Oxford people know Dr Collins well. She answers their questions every week in the *Oxford Post*.

'We're sorry Dr Collins is leaving,' says Dr Leighton, 'but we need doctors at our clinic, not writers.'

Barbara Collins' face is red. 'What's all this?' she asks angrily. 'I know nothing about this. You take away my job and you tell the *Oxford Post* first, not me.'

'Barbara, Barbara,' says Janet Leighton. She puts up a hand. 'Stop. You know that the clinic needs money. And you're expensive.'

'It's not the money, is it?' says Barbara.

'I'm sorry?' says Janet.

'It's not the money, it's the writing,' says Barbara. 'I write for the *Oxford Post* and you don't like that.'

'What are you talking about?' asks Janet.

'There can't be two famous people at the Leighton Clinic,' says Barbara, 'can there? There can only be one. You.'

Janet says nothing.

'I hate you,' says Barbara. She puts the paper on the table, then turns and leaves the room.

Chapter 3   *Friday 26 July: 9.00 am*

'Thank you for talking to us, Dr Collins,' says Williams. 'Tell me – are you the only person to hate Dr Leighton?'

Barbara laughs. 'No, Inspector. No,' she says. 'Not at all.'

Williams and Miller say nothing. They wait for Barbara Collins to speak again.

'There's her husband.' She laughs again. 'Of course, he doesn't live with her now. And her son.'

Williams and Miller leave.

On the street Miller asks, 'Where now?'

'Elizabeth Morgan, the lawyer, first,' says Williams. 'Then the husband and son.'

Chapter 4   *Thursday 25 July: 11.00 am*

Elizabeth Morgan's story

'Do sit down, Dr Leighton,' says Elizabeth Morgan. Elizabeth Morgan and Janet Leighton are in a room at Morgan and Freebody Lawyers on Worcester Street.

'Thank you,' says Janet.

'You want to talk to me about your will?' asks Elizabeth.

'Yes,' says Janet. 'I want to change my will. I don't want to leave any of my money to my son or my husband.'

Elizabeth thinks for a minute and then speaks.

'Dr Leighton, you have the house in St John Street, and your clinic on Banbury Road, ... that's about £2,000,000.'

'I know,' says Janet. 'I want it all to go to HALO – the Help Africa Live Organisation. They put money and doctors into Africa.'

'And for your son and your husband?' asks Elizabeth.

'Nothing,' says Janet.

'But Dr Leighton ...' starts Elizabeth.

'Nothing,' says Janet again. 'Nothing at all. And I want to see my new will on Monday morning.'

Chapter 5 *Friday 26 July: 10.00 am*

'Thank you for your time, Ms Morgan,' says Williams. 'Tell me – Dr Leighton's husband and son – where do they live?'

'Her husband, Simon, lives on Bridge Street, near the station,' says Morgan. 'Number 10. The son is a student. He has a room in a house on Woodstock Road. Number 177, I think.'

Williams looks at Miller. 'OK, Bridge Street next. I want to talk to Simon Leighton first.'

Chapter 6 *Thursday 25 July: 6.30 pm*

Simon Leighton's story

It's six thirty in the evening. Janet Leighton opens the front door of her house in St John Street. Her husband, Simon, is there.

'Hello, Janet,' he says.

'What do you want?' asks Janet.

'I want my money. I don't live with you now, but I am your husband. You've got all our money and our house,' says Simon.

'Come in, Simon,' says Janet. 'Then we can talk about it.'

'You always want to talk about it,' says Simon. 'This time I don't want to talk. I just want the money or the house.'

Janet looks at her husband and says nothing.

'Come on,' says Simon. 'Give me my money.'

Janet's mouth smiles, but not her eyes.

'I can't,' she says. 'I don't have it. It's all in the clinic.'

'OK, Janet,' says Simon. 'I'm going to see my lawyer.'

Janet laughs. 'Go then,' she says. 'See your lawyer. But you're not going to get any money from me.'

Then she laughs again.

Simon Leighton says nothing. His eyes are dark. He turns and walks away.

Williams and Miller leave Simon Leighton's house at eleven o'clock. They drive down the Woodstock Road again and stop in front of a big house. A young man is walking down the street. He turns into Number 177. He looks like his father.

Williams gets out of the car.

'Chris Leighton?' he asks.

'Who are you?' asks the young man.

'Inspector Williams, Oxford police. I want to talk to you.'

Chapter 8 *Thursday 25 July: 8.30 pm*

Chris Leighton's story

It's eight thirty in the evening and Chris Leighton is at his mother's house. He and his mother are drinking coffee and eating cake.

'Chris,' says Janet Leighton, 'when are you going to get a job?'

'Come on, Mum,' he answers. 'Not this again. I'm a student. I like being a student. I don't have time to work.'

'You're twenty-eight, Chris,' says Janet. 'You can't always be a student. You need a job.'

Chris drinks some coffee. Then he looks at his mother and smiles. 'I want to buy a car, Mum. Can I have £500?'

Janet looks at her son. Her eyes are cold.

'Not from me,' she says. 'I always help you with money, but now I'm stopping.'

Chris stops smiling.

'Come on, Mum,' he says. 'I need a car and it's only £500.'

'Then get a job. Or ask your father. But of course he never has any money,' says Janet.

Chris says nothing. He looks at the papers on the table in front of him. At first he doesn't read them, but then he sees something – a letter. He starts reading.

'What's this?' he asks.

Janet goes across the room and takes the letter from him.

'It's nothing to do with you,' she says.

'It's from your lawyer,' says Chris. 'It's about your will.'

'It's nothing to do with you,' says Janet again.

'Come on, Mum. Who's going to get your money? Me and Dad? Or are you changing your will?'

'Yes, I'm changing my will,' says Janet. 'I'm not going to leave anything to you or your father.'

Chris sits for a minute, mouth open. 'Nothing for me!' he says angrily. 'But I'm your son.'

'Chris, you're twenty-eight,' says Janet. 'I'm not giving you any more money. Not now. And not when I die.'

'But ...' says Chris.

'I'm going to leave my money to HALO – the Help Africa Live Organisation,' says Janet. 'They help people in Africa with money and doctors.'

Chris gets up.

'How can you leave me nothing?' he asks. 'It's because you don't love me. Well, that's OK. I don't love you.'

And he walks quickly out of the room.

Chapter 9

Friday 26 July: 12.30 pm

Williams and Miller leave Chris Leighton at twelve thirty. They drive to St Aldate's police station and go up to Inspector Williams' room. Jenkins, the police scientist, comes in with some photos.

'The photos, Inspector,' he says.

'Thank you.' Williams looks at the photos. He finds one of the Chinese dog.

'I like dogs,' he says. 'They're very good at helping people.'

Williams smiles at Miller and gives her the photo.

'Take this to the Ashmolean Museum. Speak to Dr Fischer. He's a friend. Give him the photo. Ask him, "How much money can Inspector Williams get for this dog?" And then call me with the answer.'

'OK.' Miller takes the photo and leaves.

Jenkins then gives Williams some papers.

'Fingerprints,' he says. 'But no fingerprints at all on the knife. Dr Leighton's are everywhere of course, and her husband's are ...'

'How do you know his fingerprints?' asks Williams quickly.

'They're on the police computer,' answers Jenkins, 'from his schooldays. But only for taking some jeans from a shop.'

Williams looks at the photos again. He finds one of the coffee table. He gives it to Jenkins.

'Whose fingerprints are on that book on the table, *Our Beautiful World*?' Williams asks.

Jenkins finds the right paper. 'Dr Leighton's, Simon Leighton's, and a third person's. We don't know whose.'

'Someone from the bookshop maybe?' says Williams. 'But Simon Leighton's fingerprints are on it, you say?'

'Yes, Inspector, they are,' says Jenkins.

'That's very interesting,' says Williams. 'Good work, Jenkins.'

Just then Williams' phone rings. It's Sergeant Miller.

'The dog, Inspector,' she starts, 'it's Chinese. And very old. Dr Fischer likes it very much. He says you can get about £100,000 for it.'

Williams smiles quickly. Then he looks out of the window and starts thinking.

'OK, Miller,' he tells her. 'I want you to get Dr Collins. I'm going to get Dr Leighton's husband and her son. Meet me at the house on St John Street.'

Chapter 10 *Thursday 25 July: 10.30 pm*

A death in Oxford

'You again!' says Janet Leighton.

Simon Leighton walks quickly into the house.

'My money or the house,' he says again, angrily.

He walks across the room. He takes a book off the table and looks at it.

'You have money for new books, I see,' says Simon.

He turns to his wife.

'You know my answer,' she says. 'There's no money for you. There's never going to be any money. I'm changing my will.'

'What?' Simon's eyes go dark. He puts the book down. He sees a knife on the table next to it. He takes it in his hand.

'No, you're not,' he says angrily.

Simon Leighton thinks fast. His wife, Janet, is dead. Some time the police are going to come.

'How are the police going to see this?' he thinks. 'What can I do? Yes! I know. Maybe someone comes to the front door. They want to take money, or things to sell. But Janet tries to stop them.'

Simon puts papers and books everywhere. He takes the computer from the table. He can take that away. He breaks the phone and the window. What about the Chinese dog? No, he isn't going to break that. No-one knows about the Chinese dog – just Janet and him.

Chapter 11 *Friday 26 July: 2.00 pm*

'Yes, the Chinese dog, Mr Leighton,' says Williams. 'Look at the window. Look at the phone. But the Chinese dog is OK. Why? Because it's a £100,000 Chinese dog.'

Simon Leighton's mouth opens. He looks at his son, then at Barbara Collins, then at the Inspector again.

'Your fingerprints are everywhere in this room,' says Williams. 'Do you come here often?'

'From time to time,' says Simon.

'And yesterday?' asks Williams. 'Thursday?'

'No,' says Simon. 'No.'

Williams takes the book, *Our Beautiful World*, off the coffee table. 'Your fingerprints are on this book,' he says. He takes a small bag from his jacket. Inside the bag is the receipt. 'And this is from the shop. It says 25 July. Your fingerprints are on the book from yesterday evening.'

'But …' Simon's mouth opens and closes again. He says nothing. He thinks. He looks at Williams and at Miller. Then he speaks. 'Yes, Inspector, they're my fingerprints, but …'

'And Dr Leighton's computer?' asks Miller. 'Is it at your house?'

Simon says nothing for a minute. Then he laughs.

'OK. You're right,' he says. 'But I'm happy. She's dead and I'm happy.'

Williams looks at Miller. 'Take him away,' he says.

Miller and Simon Leighton leave the room. Williams looks at Chris Leighton and Barbara Collins.

'Her husband is happy,' he says. 'Is anyone sad, do you think?'

'I'm sorry,' says Chris. 'Sorry, but not sad.'

'Her clinic helps a lot of people,' says Barbara. 'It does good work too, but no, I'm not sad.'

Williams puts the book down on the table.

'*Our Beautiful World*,' he says. 'Not really, is it?'

Then he walks out of the house.